Serving with a
Heart Like Jesus!

PRESENTED TO

John + Susan

FROM

Childrens Ministry

for SERVING
with a Heart Like Jesus!

I thank my God every time I remember you.
In all my prayers for all of you, I always
pray with joy because of your partnership in the
gospel from the first day until now.
PHILIPPIANS 1:3–5

Happy Easter
2015

www.CTAinc.com

Thanking God for Your Servant Heart!
Jane L. Fryar

ISBN 0-9747923-4-9

PRINTED IN THAILAND

Thanking God

for Your

Servant Heart!

Jane L. Fryar

The Son of Man did not come to be served, but to serve, and to give his life as a ransom for many.

MATTHEW 20:28

THANK YOU!

... The hearts you've touched.
... The wisdom you've shared.
... The support you've given.
... The tears you've dried.
... The love you've shown.

All of these reveal the ways the Lord Jesus has been at work in you, shaping and forming your heart so that it conforms more and more closely to the contours of his own heart.

Jesus served us by pouring out his life's blood on the cross for our sins. His service frees us to childlike, self-forgetful joy in serving others.

We love because he loved.

We give because he gave.

We serve because he served —
because he loved, served,
and gave himself for us!

[Jesus said,]
"For [your] sake I consecrate myself.

JOHN 17:19 ESV

Whatever you do, work at it with all your heart, as working for the Lord, not for men, since you know that you will receive an inheritance from the Lord as a reward. It is the Lord Christ you are serving.

COLOSSIANS 3:23-24

Willing

SERVICE

WHEN THE HOLY SPIRIT

repeats himself — three times — we do well to pay extra attention! Matthew, Mark, and Luke — all three — include in their gospels the same snapshot from Jesus' early ministry:

Simon's mother-in-law lay ill with a fever, and immediately they told [Jesus] about her. And he came and took her by the hand and lifted her up, and the fever left her, and she began to serve them.

MARK 1:30-31 ESV

SEE ALSO MATTHEW 8:14-15 AND LUKE 4:38-39.

Moved with compassion, Jesus takes the sufferer by the hand. His touch heals her. His touch stirs such love and faith in her heart that she, in turn, rises to serve both Christ and his followers.

No coercion here! Only the Savior's spontaneous, willing care evoking a response of authentic, willing service!

May the Holy Spirit open our hearts to an ever-deepening touch of Jesus' healing and compassion! And may we respond in ever more eager and joyful service!

Greater love has no one than this, that someone lays down his life for his friends. You are my friends if you do what I command you.

No longer do I call you servants, for the servant does not know what his master is doing; but I have called you friends, for all that I have heard from my Father I have made known to you.

You did not choose me, but I chose you and appointed you that you should go and bear fruit and that your fruit should abide.

JOHN 15:13-16 ESV

THANK YOU

for

SERVING

with a

Willing

HEART,

—A HEART—

LIKE JESUS!

I am among you as one who serves.

LUKE 22:27

*N*o one takes [my life] from me,
but I lay it down of my own accord.

JOHN 10:18 ESV

You were called to freedom. ...
Through love serve one another.

GALATIANS 5:13 ESV

Loving SERVICE

*T*HE DIFFERENCE BETWEEN *servitude* and *servanthood* is the difference between *have to* and *get to.*

Servitude is imposed from the outside; servanthood grows from an inner identity, a core commitment to do what's best for those I serve.

Jesus' death on the cross illustrates true servanthood. Scripture tells us that he gave up his life for us "of [his] own accord." The sinless Son of God freely laid down his life so that we could receive the gift of eternal life — life forever with him.

Jesus loved. And in love, he served.

Jesus' followers, in turn, served him and one another with hearts inspired, hearts set ablaze by his love. They served with a heart like Jesus' own heart. Some led and some followed, but all did what they did with servant's hearts.

May the Holy Spirit open our eyes to see Jesus' love in all its splendor! And may that love inspire us in more loving service!

As the Father has loved me, so have I loved you.
Now remain in my love.

JOHN 15:9

THANK YOU
for
SERVING
with a
Loving
H E A R T ,
— A   H E A R T —
LIKE JESUS!

[Jesus] said to all, "If anyone would come after me, let him deny himself and take up his cross daily and follow me. For whoever would save his life will lose it, but whoever loses his life for my sake will save it."

LUKE 9:23–24 ESV

Powerlessness and humility in the spiritual life do not refer to people who have no spine and who let everyone else make decisions for them. They refer to people who are so deeply in love with Jesus that they are ready to follow him wherever he guides them, always trusting that, with him, they will find life and find it abundantly.

HENRI NOUWEN, 1989

Courageous

SERVICE

*I*N A DAY WHEN the Roman government used crucifixion as a terrorist weapon to stifle rebellion in the territories it occupied, Jesus' warning about "taking up the cross" surely shocked his hearers!

But Jesus never hid the truth from his followers; he was no spin doctor, shading the facts to manipulate the faithful. No, Jesus rebuked, warned, taught, and comforted them — all this in the context of an authentic, personal relationship with each individual. In Jesus' name, the apostle Paul urges us likewise to "[speak] the truth in love" (EPHESIANS 4:15).

Silence carries a high price tag — both for individuals and organizations. It imposes a heavy psychological tax on the person who chooses to ignore a critical issue. It blunts the creative edge of organizations. It limits any group's effectiveness. It's easy to understand why Paul called for truth.

Note, though, that Paul does not call for naked truth, but rather for truth spoken in love. Peter, John, Martha, Mary Magdalene, and the rest were able to hear and apply the truth Jesus spoke because they knew he truly cared about them. He said what he said not to hurt, but to help.

May the Holy Spirit continually encourage our hearts in the love our Savior has for us. And may we, in turn, develop ever-deepening courage and integrity so that we speak the truth in love to those who serve with us.

[May we] no longer be children, tossed to and fro by the waves and carried about by every wind of doctrine, by human cunning, by craftiness in deceitful schemes.

Rather, speaking the truth in love, we are to grow up in every way into him who is the head, into Christ, from whom the whole body, joined and held together by every joint with which it is equipped, when each part is working properly, makes the body grow so that it builds itself up in love.

EPHESIANS 4:14–16 ESV

THANK YOU

for

SERVING

with a

Courageous

HEART,

—A HEART—

LIKE JESUS!

Now before the Feast of the Passover, when Jesus knew that his hour had come to depart out of this world to the Father, having loved his own who were in the world, he loved them to the end. ...

Jesus, knowing that the Father had given all things into his hands, and that he had come from God and was going back to God, rose from supper. He laid aside his outer garments, and taking a towel, tied it around his waist. Then he poured water into a basin and began to wash the disciples' feet and to wipe them with the towel that was wrapped around him.

JOHN 13:1-5 ESV

God determines your greatness by how many people you serve, not how many people serve you.

RICK WARREN, 2002

Humble

SERVICE

*R*espected scholar and organizational theorist Jim Collins has studied what it takes to move an organization from good to great and keep it there — over decades. One key finding involves what Collins calls "Level 5 leadership."

When level 5 leaders come to the crossroads of a difficult decision, they consistently exercise the humility of self-forgetfulness and focus on the mission of the organization. Over time, this kind of leadership transforms organizations.

On the night before he died, Jesus took on the chore of washing the disciples' feet, ordinarily the task of the lowliest household slave. In this act, he continued the pattern of service he had followed throughout his ministry.

For us, as for Christ, true humility involves, not self-deprecation or self-criticism, but rather self-forgetfulness — the kind of self-forgetfulness that focuses on doing the heavenly Father's will, on sharing the heavenly Father's forgiving love.

Because Christ conquered the power of sin when he died and came back to life, we can exercise, in true humility, true service.

May the Holy Spirit impress upon our hearts the meaning of Christ's service for us. And may we, in turn, worship him as we humbly serve his people.

God has called you to a free life. ...
Use your freedom to serve one another in love.

GALATIANS 5:13 THE MESSAGE

THANK YOU
for
SERVING
with a
Humble
HEART,
—A HEART—
LIKE JESUS!

[Jesus said,] "I am among you as the one who serves."

LUKE 22:27 ESV

What we *do* for Christ grows out of
who we *are* in Christ!

Authentic

SERVICE

IMAGINE A LUMP OF

LIFELESS CLAY lying on the ground outside
an artist's studio. Watch as the artist scoops it up and slaps it on
his potter's wheel. As the wheel begins to spin, slowly at first and
then at a brisker clip, the lump becomes a useful vessel.

A work of art slowly emerges from beneath the potter's hands.
The potter moves one thumb ever so slightly, and the vessel
takes on a unique shape, a shape perfectly suited to the potter's
purposes. Minutes or hours later, the artist steps back to admire his
masterpiece.

The prophet Jeremiah used this image as a metaphor for the lives
of God's people. (SEE JEREMIAH 18:1-6.) In our Lord's hands, our
lives of service take shape. We become his work of art, vessels
uniquely suited for specific purposes.

What we *do* for Christ grows out of who we *are* in Christ. The
more closely our actions match our core identity as Jesus' redeemed
people, the more authentic — and genuinely helpful — the service
we render.

*May we submit gladly and willingly to the Spirit's gentle shaping of our hearts so
that our service flows ever more authentically from a heart like Christ's own heart!*

That we ... *might BE for the praise of his glory.*

EPHESIANS 1:12 *(emphasis added)*

THANK YOU
for
SERVING
from an
Authentic
H E A R T,
—A HEART—
LIKE JESUS!

From this time many of his disciples turned back and no longer followed him.

"You do not want to leave too, do you?"
Jesus asked the Twelve.

Simon Peter answered him, "Lord, to whom shall we go? You have the words of eternal life. We believe and know that you are the Holy One of God."

JOHN 6:66-69

Power offers an easy substitute for the hard task of love. It seems easier to be God than to love God, easier to control people than to love people, easier to own life than to love life.

HENRI NOUWEN, 1989

Influential
SERVICE

AN OLD STORY TELLS OF rivalry between Sun and Wind. Each claimed to be the stronger, until one day Sun challenged Wind to a contest: Who could more quickly get an old man to remove his coat?

Wind blew fierce and cold, then fiercer and colder still, but the old man merely pulled his coat more tightly around himself. Then Sun went to work. The air grew warmer, the path the man walked, softer. Before long, off came the coat.

Influencers don't bluster and blow. They understand that coercion has limited power. Heartfelt service, on the other hand, has nearly limitless power to produce positive change.

Jesus chose the power of service, the power of influence. He forced no one to walk with him; in fact, Scripture tells us that some early followers later walked away. But in the end, what seemed to be Christ's weakness — his voluntary service on our behalf — secured eternal life for millions of believers down through cascades of generations.

May the Holy Spirit convince us continually to renounce the temptation to control or manipulate others, and may he create in its place the gentle desire to serve and sway others through our Christlike service.

Be imitators of God, therefore, as dearly loved children and live a life of love, just as Christ loved us and gave himself up for us as a fragrant offering and sacrifice to God.

EPHESIANS 5:1-2

THANK YOU

for

SERVING

with an

Influential

HEART,

—A HEART—

LIKE JESUS!

[Jesus] went out to the mountain to pray, and all night he continued in prayer to God.

LUKE 6:12 ESV

Fear not because your prayer is stammering, your words feeble, and your language poor. Jesus can understand you. Just as a mother understands the first lisping of her infant, so does the blessed Savior understand sinners. He can read a sigh, and see a meaning in a groan.

J. C. RYLE

Prayerful
SERVICE

THE CREATOR OF OUR

UNIVERSE, the Commander of heaven's angel army, fell on his face in Gethsemane. Jesus poured out "loud cries and tears to him who was able to save him from death," and, the Bible says, "he was heard because of his reverence." (HEBREWS 5:7 ESV).

Despite the divine rights he could have claimed, our Savior came to his heavenly Father on his knees, on his face — in utter dependence — submitting fully to the Father's will. *A prayerful heart is a reverent, humble heart.*

Despite the agonies that lay ahead, Jesus prayed in childlike trust, relying on the Father's love and on his promise to release death's bitter grip at the proper time. *A prayerful heart is a trusting heart.*

We who serve God's people today sometimes struggle to surrender to the Father's will for the lives of those we serve, let alone for our own lives. We sometimes question the Father's wisdom and doubt his love.

Through his cross may Jesus pardon our self-reliance and fretfulness, working in each of us a reverent, trusting, prayerful heart.

We give thanks to God always for all of you, constantly mentioning you in our prayers, remembering before our God and Father your work of faith and labor of love and steadfastness of hope in our Lord Jesus Christ.

1 THESSALONIANS 1:2-3 ESV

THANK YOU
for
SERVING
with a
Prayerful
HEART,
—A HEART—
LIKE JESUS!

[Jesus] said, "For the Son of Man came to seek and to save what was lost."

LUKE 19:10

Nobody made a greater mistake than he who did nothing because he could do only a little.

EDMUND BURKE

Zealous
SERVICE

A STREAM WITHOUT BANKS
quickly grows into a very large puddle. Banks provide boundaries
and make it possible for a river to flow freely and purposefully
within those boundaries.

What is your life about? What is your organization up to? Call it
a purpose. Call it a vision. Call it a preferred future state. Whatever
you call it, your vision channels your energy. Your vision sets
boundaries and provides focus. Without a clear mission, passion
dissolves and zeal quickly evaporates. Put another way, those who
try to do everything accomplish little or nothing.

Jesus focused on a single purpose. He described that purpose in
the phrase *to seek and to save what is lost.* We were the objects of his
search. We were the objects of his attention, his focus. Zealous
and passionate, Jesus came after us in our sin and rebellion.

More than simply seeking us, Jesus saved us. The Suffering Servant
died our death in our place. He rose again from death to give us
life forever.

*May the Holy Spirit sharpen our vision, granting us passion for his purposes. May
we serve our Servant-King with zealous hearts, hearts on fire with love for him and
for those he still seeks.*

*T*each me your way, O LORD,
    that I may walk in your truth;
    unite my heart to fear your name.

PSALM 86:11 ESV

THANK YOU
for
SERVING
with a
Zealous
H E A R T ,
— A H E A R T —
LIKE JESUS!

*Let us not grow weary of doing good, for in due
season we will reap, if we do not give up. So then, as we
have opportunity, let us do good to everyone,
and especially to those who are of the household of faith.*

GALATIANS 6:9–10 ESV

*The grace of our Lord was poured out on me abundantly,
along with the faith and love that are in Christ Jesus.*

1 TIMOTHY 1:14

Faithful
SERVICE

*T*HE LIVING GOD. The Scriptures use this name to distinguish between the true God and all false gods. It implies both power and willingness to act; the Living God moves on the behalf of his people. Idols, in contrast:

> *… have mouths, but cannot speak,*
> *eyes, but they cannot see;*
> *they have ears, but cannot hear,*
> *nor is there breath in their mouths.*
>
> PSALM 135:16-17

Ultimately, God acted for us in his Son, Christ Jesus — in the perfect life Jesus lived in our place, in the agony of the death Jesus died for our sins. Now Jesus tells us:

> *"Do not be afraid. … I am the Living One;*
> *I was dead, and behold I am alive for ever and ever!*
> *And I hold the keys of death and Hades."*
>
> REVELATION 1:17-18

This Living Christ still acts today on our behalf and on the behalf of those we serve in his name. We may see results right now — or not. We may feel we're getting somewhere — or not. But no matter what we see or feel, Jesus *is* at work. We have his Word of promise!

May the Holy Spirit fill our hearts with faith that holds onto God's strong promises and continues to speak his Word faithfully.

*A*s *the rain and the snow*
come down from heaven,
and do not return to it
without watering the earth
and making it bud and flourish,
so that it yields seed for the sower and
bread for the eater,
so is my word that goes out from my mouth:

It will not return to me empty,
but will accomplish what I desire
and achieve the purpose for which I sent it.

ISAIAH 55:10-11

THANK YOU
for
SERVING
with a
Faithful
HEART,
—A HEART—
LIKE JESUS!

Because so many people were coming and going that they did not even have a chance to eat, [Jesus] said to [the disciples], "Come with me by yourselves to a quiet place and get some rest."

MARK 6:31

There are not three levels of spiritual life — worship, waiting, and work. Yet some of us seem to jump like spiritual frogs from worship to waiting, and from waiting to work. God's idea is that the three should go together as one.

OSWALD CHAMBERS

Sacrificial SERVICE

"**ALL YOUR TIME IS THIS CHURCH'S TIME!**" scowled the deacon over his reading glasses at the new youth worker.

Maybe you've met this deacon! If so, you may need God's Sabbath rest!

God gave ancient Israel one day off each week to rest, to worship, and to love their families and friends. The nations around Israel thought them lazy in this regard. Those outside God's covenant had to slave seven days a week just to keep the wolf from the door!

The Sabbath was a gift of rest, given like a wedding ring, as it were, to signify the Lord's love. It sealed his promise to provide for his people.

All our time does indeed belong to the Lord Jesus. We will one day give an account for how we've spent it, invested it, or wasted it. But in Christ Jesus, Israel's God is our God, too. Sometimes he calls us to go the extra mile, to do the extra task. But just as surely he also calls us aside to rest, to eat, to let him refresh us.

May we hear the Lord Jesus calling us, whether to work or to rest, and respond to that call with hearts filled with love and trust in him!

[Jesus said,]"Come to me, all you who are weary and burdened, and I will give you rest."

MATTHEW 11:28

THANK YOU

for

SERVING

from a

Sacrificial, Rested

HEART,

—A HEART—

LIKE JESUS!

*N*ehemiah said, "Go and enjoy choice food and sweet drinks, and send some to those who have nothing prepared. This day is sacred to our Lord. Do not grieve, for the joy of the LORD is your strength."

NEHEMIAH 8:10

*T*he fruit of the Spirit is love, joy, peace.

GALATIANS 5:22

Joyful
SERVICE

Nehemiah's people shouldered heavy burdens. Baked by the searing sun, a brick in one hand and sword in the other, the workers kept a wary eye out for ambush by their ever-present enemies. Stone by stone, they built the wall of Jerusalem. They slept in their clothes, but not very deeply.

Finally, it was done. The priests organized a service of thanksgiving, but as the assembly heard God's Word, their relief turned to deep repentance. Tears flowed freely as the people remembered the LORD's goodness to them despite their complaining and faithlessness.

Those who serve on heaven's "construction sites" today do so with an awareness of the dangers sin and Satan pose. We, too, struggle to get a good night's sleep when those we serve face temptation or trouble. God's Word of law often brings tears to our eyes as we recognize our own shortcomings.

If you stand with Nehemiah amidst the rubble right now, if your eyes brim with tears of contrition over your own disobedience, then let your Savior quiet your heart with his pardon and peace. Hear his words of comfort: "Do not grieve, for the joy of the LORD is your strength" (NEHEMIAH 8:10).

May the joy of our forgiving Lord strengthen our hearts, as Jesus renews us for today's tasks.

Restore to me the joy of your salvation,
and uphold me with a willing spirit.

Then I will teach transgressors your ways,
and sinners will return to you.

PSALM 51:12-13 ESV

THANK YOU
for
SERVING
with a
Joyful
HEART,
—A HEART—
LIKE JESUS!

You turned to God from idols to serve the living and true God, and to wait for his Son from heaven, whom he raised from the dead, Jesus who delivers us from the wrath to come.

1 THESSALONIANS 1:9–10 ESV

Are [the angels] not all ministering spirits sent out to serve for the sake of those who are to inherit salvation?

HEBREWS 1:14 ESV

Eternal

SERVICE

OUR LADY OF PERPETUAL RESPONSIBILITY.

Humorist Garrison Keillor hung this name ruefully on one of the churches in his fictitious village, Lake Wobegon.

No matter what the name of our church, the blessing of being able to serve can become a burden unless we see those we serve through heaven's eyes, as:

- *Sons and daughters of heaven's High King!*
- *Sisters and brothers of the Lord Jesus!*
- *Heirs of God, co-heirs with Christ!*

Yes, they still struggle with sin. So do we. Yes, they still fall for Satan's temptations. So do we. Yes, they often seem unthankful. So do we. But one day, they will shine in glory — just as we will — trophies of God's grace in Christ!

That eternal perspective transforms our service. It energizes our calling. Even the most menial tasks, done in Jesus' name, matter. They matter forever!

"He is no fool who gives what he cannot keep to gain what he cannot lose," wrote missionary Jim Elliot in his journal sometime before his martyrdom in 1956.

May the Holy Spirit develop in our hearts an eternal perspective as we contemplate our service for the Lord Jesus. May he make us diligent and watchful as we work and wait for his return.

*T*hen one of the elders asked me, "These in white robes—who are they, and where did they come from?" …

And he said, "These are they who have come out of the great tribulation; they have washed their robes and made them white in the blood of the Lamb.

Therefore,

"they are before the throne of God
and serve him day and night in his temple;
and he who sits on the throne will spread his tent
over them. …

The Lamb at the center of the throne will be their shepherd;
he will lead them to springs of living water.
And God will wipe away every tear from their eyes."

REVELATION 7:13–17

THANK YOU
for
SERVING
with a
HEART
fixed on eternity,
—A HEART—
LIKE JESUS!

Well done, my good servant!

LUKE 19:17